P9-DNM-186

Put Beginning Readers on the Right Track with
ALL ABOARD READING™

The All Aboard Reading series is especially designed for beginning readers. Written by noted authors and illustrated in full color, these are books that children really want to read—books to excite their imagination, expand their interests, make them laugh, and support their feelings. With fiction and nonfiction stories that are high interest and curriculum-related, All Aboard Reading books offer something for every young reader. And with four different reading levels, the All Aboard Reading series lets you choose which books are most appropriate for your children and their growing abilities.

Picture Readers
Picture Readers have super-simple texts, with many nouns appearing as rebus pictures. At the end of each book are 24 flash cards—on one side is a rebus picture; on the other side is the written-out word.

Station Stop 1
Station Stop 1 books are best for children who have just begun to read. Simple words and big type make these early reading experiences more comfortable. Picture clues help children to figure out the words on the page. Lots of repetition throughout the text helps children to predict the next word or phrase—an essential step in developing word recognition.

Station Stop 2
Station Stop 2 books are written specifically for children who are reading with help. Short sentences make it easier for early readers to understand what they are reading. Simple plots and simple dialogue help children with reading comprehension.

Station Stop 3
Station Stop 3 books are perfect for children who are reading alone. With longer text and harder words, these books appeal to children who have mastered basic reading skills. More complex stories captivate children who are ready for more challenging books.

In addition to All Aboard Reading books, look for All Aboard Math Readers™ (fiction stories that teach math concepts children are learning in school); All Aboard Science Readers™ (nonfiction books that explore the most fascinating science topics in age-appropriate language); All Aboard Poetry Readers™ (funny, rhyming poems for readers of all levels); and All Aboard Mystery Readers™ (puzzling tales where children piece together evidence with the characters).

All Aboard for happy reading!

Chase Branch Library
17731 W. Seven Mile Rd.
Detroit, MI 48235

DEC 08

CH

For my brother, Chip, who always
stands up for what he believes—A.J.P.

To Jackie Robinson, for breaking the barrier—R.C.

GROSSET & DUNLAP
Published by the Penguin Group
Penguin Group (USA) Inc., 375 Hudson Street, New York, New York 10014, USA
Penguin Group (Canada), 90 Eglinton Avenue East, Suite 700, Toronto, Ontario
M4P 2Y3, Canada (a division of Pearson Penguin Canada Inc.)
Penguin Books Ltd., 80 Strand, London WC2R 0RL, England
Penguin Group Ireland, 25 St. Stephen's Green, Dublin 2, Ireland
(a division of Penguin Books Ltd.)
Penguin Group (Australia), 250 Camberwell Road, Camberwell, Victoria
3124, Australia (a division of Pearson Australia Group Pty. Ltd.)
Penguin Books India Pvt. Ltd., 11 Community Centre, Panchsheel Park,
New Delhi—110 017, India
Penguin Group (NZ), 67 Apollo Drive, Rosedale, North Shore 0745,
Auckland, New Zealand (a division of Pearson New Zealand Ltd.)
Penguin Books (South Africa) (Pty.) Ltd., 24 Sturdee Avenue,
Rosebank, Johannesburg 2196, South Africa

Penguin Books Ltd., Registered Offices:
80 Strand, London WC2R 0RL, England

The scanning, uploading, and distribution of this book via the Internet or via any other means
without the permission of the publisher is illegal and punishable by law. Please purchase only
authorized electronic editions, and do not participate in or encourage electronic piracy of
copyrighted materials. Your support of the author's rights is appreciated.

Photo credits: page 3: ©MLB Photos via Getty Images; page 6: © Bettmann/CORBIS; page 18:
© Associated Press; page 27: © Associated Press; page 28: © Associated Press; page 40:
© Bettmann/CORBIS; page 44: © Associated Press; page 45: © Associated Press;
page 46: © Associated Press; page 47: © Associated Press; page 48: © Bettman/CORBIS.

Text copyright © 2008 by April Jones Prince. Illustrations copyright © 2008 by Robert Casilla.
All rights reserved. Published by Grosset & Dunlap, a division of Penguin Young Readers
Group, 345 Hudson Street, New York, New York 10014. ALL ABOARD READING and
GROSSET & DUNLAP are trademarks of Penguin Group (USA) Inc. Printed in the U.S.A.

Library of Congress Cataloging-in-Publication Data

Prince, April Jones.
Jackie Robinson : he led the way / by April Jones Prince ; illustrated by Robert Casilla.
p. cm. -- (All aboard reading. Station stop 2)
ISBN 978-0-448-44721-6 (pbk.)
1. Robinson, Jackie, 1919-1972--Juvenile literature. 2. Baseball players--United States--
Biography--Juvenile literature. 3. African American baseball players--Biography--Juvenile
literature. I. Casilla, Robert, ill. II. Title.
GV865.R6P75 2008
796.357092--dc22
[B]
2007015503

ISBN 978-0-448-44721-6   10 9 8 7 6 5 4 3 2

Jackie Robinson
He Led the Way

By April Jones Prince
Illustrated by Robert Casilla
with photographs

Grosset & Dunlap

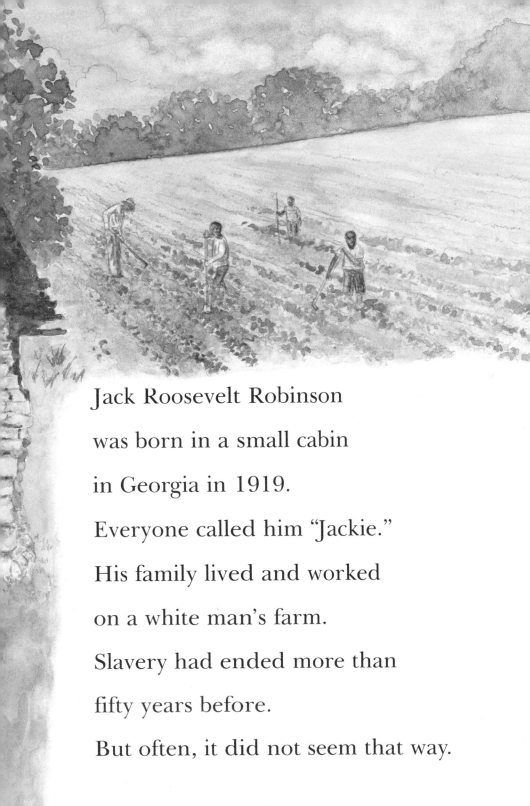

Jack Roosevelt Robinson
was born in a small cabin
in Georgia in 1919.
Everyone called him "Jackie."
His family lived and worked
on a white man's farm.
Slavery had ended more than
fifty years before.
But often, it did not seem that way.

Black children could not go to school
with white children.

Black families could not eat in restaurants with white people or stay at the same hotels.

They had to sit in the back

of public buses . . .

. . . and in the worst seats

at ballparks.

One day, Jackie Robinson

would help

change all this.

He did it through baseball.

Jackie's family moved to
Pasadena, California,
when he was still a small boy.

They were the only black
family on their block.
And their neighbors
did not welcome them.

But Jackie's mother told her children,
"We have the same right
to live here as anyone else."
She did not want her children
looking for trouble.
But she did want them
to stick up for themselves.

One day, a girl called

Jackie mean names.

Her father threw stones at Jackie.

What did Jackie do?

He shouted names

and threw stones right back at them.

In school, Jackie did okay.

But in sports, he made magic!

Jackie always played to win—

even a game of tag.

Kids even paid Jackie
to be on their team.

All through high school and college,
Jackie played sports:

football,

baseball,

and basketball.

He set a new record for the long jump.

He was a local hero.

His name was always in the papers.

After college,

Jackie wanted to play sports for a living.

But no major team in any sport

hired black players.

There were all-black baseball teams

like the Kansas City Monarchs

and the Homestead Grays.

These teams had their own leagues.

Fans flocked to see stars like

pitcher Satchel Paige

and super-slugger Josh Gibson.

The games were fast-paced and exciting.

Jackie could play on one of these teams . . .

. . . except for one thing:

World War II had started.

Even in the U.S. army,

black soldiers

did not eat, sleep, or train

with white soldiers.

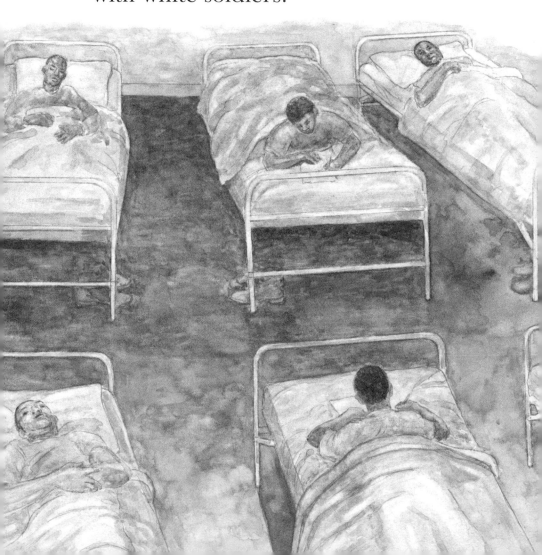

In the snack bar, only a few seats

were set aside for blacks.

"We are all in this war together,"

Jackie told the general.

"And everyone should have the

same rights."

The general agreed.

Black soldiers got more seats

in the snack bar.

After the war,

Jackie played baseball for

the Kansas City Monarchs.

But Jackie wasn't a Monarch for long.

Branch Rickey was the president

of the Brooklyn Dodgers.

He had heard about Jackie Robinson

from a scout named Clyde Sukeforth.

Just like Jackie,

Branch Rickey hated to lose.

He wanted to win a World Series.

There were so many

great black ballplayers.

Rickey thought it was time

that one of them joined the Dodgers.

Maybe Jackie Robinson.

Branch Rickey asked

Jackie Robinson

to meet him in New York.

"I want you to play

for the Dodgers,"

he told Jackie.

"You will be put down

and spit upon.

But you must not fight back!

That will make people say

that blacks don't belong

in the major leagues.

Do you have the guts to play

no matter what?"

It was not Jackie Robinson's nature

to keep quiet.

But he decided he had to.

He gave Branch Rickey his answer:

"YES."

In 1946, Jackie married
his college sweetheart, Rachel Isum.
She traveled with him to spring training
in Florida.

Jackie played his first season
on a Dodgers minor-league team.
This was like practice for
the major leagues.
As always, he played to win.
He led his league in hitting
and was tied in runs scored.
He was second in stolen bases.

So on April 15, 1947,
Jackie Robinson made history
as the first black ballplayer
in the major leagues.
He stepped onto Ebbets Field
in Brooklyn.

He was wearing a Dodgers uniform.

He was their new first baseman.

He said it was a dream come true.

Branch Rickey's warning also came true.

Once again,

people called Jackie mean names.

He got hateful letters.

At games,

pitchers on the other team

threw balls at his head on purpose.

Even many of the Dodgers
did not want him around.
Jackie took it all in silence.

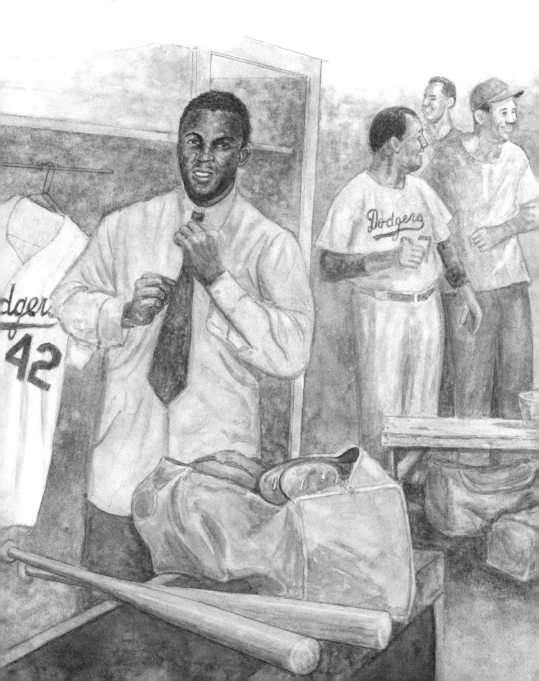

But lots of fans adored Jackie
right from the start.

His courage and flashy play
proved that blacks belonged
in the major leagues.
Jackie hit and ran as well as
the best of his white teammates.

But he had a way of stealing bases that was all his own.

Jackie could steal home plate!

He would dance
on and off third base.
Then he'd dash down
the baseline.
The next moment,
he was sliding into home plate.
Score!

Jackie was named Rookie of the Year.

By 1949,

Jackie had been

quiet long enough.

Now he spoke up

when umpires made bad calls.

And he talked back

to ballplayers

on other teams.

Jackie lost some fans.

But he was standing up

for his rights—

not just in baseball,

but in all of America.

In 1949,

he was voted

the National League's

Most Valuable Player.

It was a great honor.

Jackie deserved it.

Jackie helped the Dodgers
get to the World Series six times.
Five times, they lost.
Then, in 1955,
they finally won!
Jackie said the win was
"one of the greatest thrills
of my life."

By that time, there were almost forty black players on major-league teams. There were blacks in other pro sports, too.

Roy Campanella

Jackie Robinson had
helped change America.

Willie Mays   Hank Aaron

Jackie played in the major leagues for ten years.

Then he became a businessman.

He spent more time with Rachel and their three children.

And he kept working for

equal rights.

In 1962, Jackie was the first black man

voted into the Baseball Hall of Fame.

Jackie lived to be fifty-three.

He showed America that talent is not

based on skin color.

Jackie Robinson was a great ballplayer—

and a great American.